GOLF
and be
DAMNED

Written and Illustrated by
LAWRENCE LARIAR

Prentice-Hall, Inc. New York

LIBRARY OF CONGRESS CATALOG CARD NO: 54–9627

Books by Lawrence Lariar

Humor and Nonsense

BEST CARTOONS OF THE YEAR   CARTOONING FOR EVERYBODY

THE EASY WAY TO CARTOONING   CAREERS IN CARTOONING

BED AND BORED   YANKEE YIDDISH

OH! DR. KINSEY!   THE ARMY FUN BOOK

FISH AND BE DAMNED!   YOU'VE GOT ME IN STITCHES!

LIBERTY LAUGHS OUT LOUD   FATHER GOOSENAGLE (*with* COL. STOOPNAGLE)

Novels

THE DAY I DIED   WIN PLACE AND DIE!

FRIDAY FOR DEATH   YOU CAN'T CATCH ME

THE MAN WITH THE LUMPY NOSE   HE DIED LAUGHING

THE GIRL WITH THE FRIGHTENED EYES   RUN FOR YOUR LIFE

DEATH PAINTS THE PICTURE

On Selling

THE SALESMAN'S TREASURY

Second Printing . . . . October, 1954

CONTENTS

FOREWORD

A NOTE ON THE AUTHOR

Lawrence Lariar comes from a long line of golfing ancestors, among whom may be numbered: Antoine Niblique, Pierre Putter, Jean-Paul Slice, and an old party named Fenton K. Birdberg, who is Chief Hole Puncher at The Babbling Bromide Links, in Upper Plate, Ohio.

Lariar has devoted a small lifetime to the study of the game, from time to time contributing many new and dandy inventions for the help of the ambitious amateur. The diagram above shows Lariar's latest device (Pat. Pending), designed to assist the beginner in keeping his head down and his eye on the ball.

IT SAYS SO RIGHT HERE—
IN THE BOOK

Every spring, as soon as the violets begin to sprout along the back ridge of your mother-in-law's bonnet, the publishing world bubbles and steams with a rash of new golf tomes. Statistics show that if these books were laid end to end, they would form a straight line from The Cave of the Big Winds, in Outer Mongolia, to my wastebasket in Freeport, Long Island.

The beginning golfer (like the beginning fisherman, the beginning yachtsman and the beginning lover) assumes that he knows very little about his new-found hobby. He fumbles and gropes. He squirms and fidgets. He will grab hold of his club and waggle it in the most preposterous manner. He will flail his way around a run-of-the-mill golf course and wind up with a score of 198, a bad backache, and hot and cold running fits. This situation must run its course until the

9

unfortunate neophyte discovers the world of instruction books. From there on in, the panic begins.

His first visit to the local bookstore reveals a fifteen-foot shelf, glutted with such titles as these:

Knock Ninety Strokes Off Your Game, by Tommy Balldrash.

How to Be Happy and Play Golf While Four-Putting Seven Greens out of Ten, by Herkimer Q. Foldingback.

Famous Holes I Have Known, by John F. Sewerage.

Swing and Sing, by Florence Nightingale.

The Left Hand Is the Dreamer, by Calvin Cooledge.

The Postman Always Putts Twice, by Wm. Shakeshaft.

Start Swinging, Stop Dreaming, by Sigmund Freud.

After wandering in the murky bookstall for hours, the average myopic beginner will buy at least one volume and sneak slyly back into his garage, dragging his clubs behind him. Here he will study the book while handling his mashie, struggling desperately to imitate the fancy photographs in the volume. Despite the taunts and jibes of friends and neighbors, the hopeful amateur will spend hundreds of hours whacking away at a fluffy practice ball during the long winter months.

And in the spring?

He will emerge on the first tee and address the ball with poise and confidence, waggling his hips and adjusting his bones to imitate that wonderful instruction picture on page 207. He will next indulge in a well-grooved backswing, smooth and graceful and timed with enough perfection to make Ben Hogan drool with envy. He will then swing at the golf ball, holding his hands firm and tight, using his left hand in the approved grip, bending his elbow to the precise angle for gaining the ultimate in power. After which, the clubhead strikes the ball, and —

— the ball dribbles for a sliced fifty yards.

The immediate reaction to an experience of this type varies according to the emotional make-up of the golfer involved. The high-

Diagram of Average Golfer trying to remember average book information he has absorbed during average winter.

strung, sensitive type will usually burst into a broth of rage, fling his driver wildly into the air, and run screaming into the nearest sand trap. The intellectual and composed type will shake his head sadly, advance to the ball for the next shot and proceed to worry his way along the course for a score of 256 for the 18 holes. Other types have been known to (a) fall into a dead faint, (b) break golf clubs or, (c) kick caddies.

Yet all bookish and scholarly neophytes are blessed with one dominant trait — they forget quickly. It is this looseness in the memory department that publishers bless. Statistics prove that the average golfer will completely block out his sad experience with the first instruction book — and return once again during the following winter to purchase another dose of the same prosy cathartic. This explains the appearance, only last season, of another list of cheerful golfing guides such as:

So, You're Back Again for More Instruction, Eh?, by Lawsome Bittel.

What to Do with Broken Golf Clubs, by Mike Eisenhower.

How Green Is My Foursome?, by Zelda Twitt.

Sexual Behavior of the Masculine Golfer, by Dr. J. Wormsey.

Having suffered through at least a dozen seasons of bookish back-swings myself, the plight of my brother amateurs interests me. It's about time some pioneer came along to change the reading habits of Mr. Average Golfer and take him out of that dank garage and into the sunshine again for more fruitful winter pastimes.

For this reason, I've compiled the following instruction chapters, boiled down out of more than fifteen years of personal experience with professional manuals. Here, for the first time in the history of the game, the bumbling beginner can find practically nothing at all, complete with many diagrams that are just as worthless as the text.

A BAD APPROACH: A mashie that missed his mark.

ARE YOU MENTALLY EQUIPPED FOR PLAYING GOLF?

Experts in the field of psychiatry have long been plumbing the mysteries of what goes on in the average golfer's bag of brains. They have explored the libido, the ego, the id and the unconscious. They have dug deep into the gray mists of the psyche, on the alert for repressions, regressions, hallucinations and regurgitations. Yet, despite their scientific dredging, not one of them has yet come up with an answer to such simple questions as:

(a) Why does a normal man get pleasure out of beating the hide off a small white ball, walking an average of seven miles in pursuit of his own bad shots, wandering through swamp, mire, wood and field to end up 18 holes later with a bad score, a bad temper and a bad stabbing pain in the area of his sacroiliac?

(b) Why, after a rest of a few hours, does the same normal man repeat this nonsense?

(c) Why does this practice continue, year after year, until the above-mentioned lunatic either breaks 100, breaks his clubs, or breaks his back?

The time has come for an end to shilly-shallying answers to these problems. The latest statistics show that more than eighteen million unfortunates in this country now pursue the sport, most of whom would do better using their clubs to churn cheese.

In an effort to clear up the general confusion, I've devised a flawless test for all who would prefer to check their capabilities before further long treks through the veldt. Grab your pencil and answer these problems slowly and carefully. Try to be honest. Try to be forthright. Try to remember your past habits on the fairway. Just try, you liar, you!

Problem Number One: THE BALL IN THE ROUGH

You have hit your ball a nasty slice and finally discover it buried in a grove of swamp grass, out of sight of the other players in your foursome.

(1) Did you use your spade to hit the ball out?_____

(2) Suppose you missed? Did you try again?_____

(3) You missed it again. What now?_____

(4) How far did you throw the ball?_____

(5) Did you make the green?_____

(6) Did they believe you when you carded a 5 for the hole?_____

(7) What makes you such a terrible cheat?_____

Problem Number Two: YOUR PARTNER'S PLIGHT

You are playing a round with a strange red-headed woman who reminds you strongly of Marilyn Monroe, Lana Turner, Denise Darcel and Dagmar. She is a beginner and enjoys having you instruct her as you play. On the fourth hole, she smites her ball into a deeply wooded, lonely section of rough.

(1) Did you enter the woods with her to help her find her ball?_____

(2) After you found her ball, why did you toss it away?_____

(3) Did she see you?_____

(4) What happened after that?_____

(5) And then what? Did she slap your face?_____

(6) How much did you tip the caddies when you sent them back to the clubhouse?_____

(7) Didn't the grass get damp after dark?_____

(8) What did you tell your wife when you were late to dinner?_____

(9) How much did the divorce cost you?_____

Problem Number Three: THE URGE TO WIN

You are involved in a foursome playing a competitive game for money. The stakes are high. If you and your partner win, you make $1,000.00 each. On the eighteenth hole, your opponents can grab the game only if Jones (a notoriously bad putter) is able to sink a long and intricate putt from the edge of the green.

(1) As Jones prepared to putt, did you wish he'd throw an epileptic fit?_____

(2) When he slowly adjusted his club and started his swing, did you suddenly cough, belch, or whinny?_____

(3) Did your noise make Jones miss the cup?_____

(4) Why didn't you duck when he threw his club at you?_____

(5) Did the doctors say your brain concussion was serious?_____

(6) When do you expect to leave the hospital?_____

A FEW NOTES ON GOLFING ETIQUETTE

Speak softly — but always carry a big stick.
Frank Merriwell

The life of a golfing pundit is fraught with all manner of interesting events, including the daily trip to the mailbox. From all corners of the globe, my enthusiastic pupils keep sending evidences of their appreciation and deep affection. No longer am I surprised to see my postman stagger up to the front door loaded down with a galaxy of gifts: a covey of quail from Quincy, a vacuolated vat of hot oil from Bessarabia, or a large portion of pornographic postals from Paris, France.

Along with such burnt offerings before my personal shrine, not a week goes by without a few gross of chatty notes concerning the *"dandy game with the little white ball and the sticks."* A recent survey of my mailbags, done for me by the Mailbag Survey Company, brings to light the fact that practically everybody longs for a few simple words on the subject of Golfing Etiquette.

"When my wife plays with me," inquires Rutabaga J. Wormhole, "should I let her hit before me, play by herself, or should I simply drown her in the first water hole?"

"Which is the proper iron for beating my husband?" asks Molly Pitcher, of Black Navel, Dakota.

"Why does my boy friend get so mad when I tell him something important while he is putting?" whispers Miss Irma Sandtrap of St. Andrews, Pa.

These, and many other provoking questions, have prompted me to outline the general rules for human behavior while playing golf. The following queries and rejoinders should go a long way toward stopping the cat and dog fights on the clubhouse terrace. For further answers to other questions, simply enclose a thousand dollar bill in a plain manila wrapper and mail it at once to: The Calumny School of Golfing Etiquette, No. 10 Downing Street, London, England. If a man answers, hang up, of course.

DEPORTMENT AT THE FIRST TEE

QUESTION: Are ladies always first in a mixed foursome?

ANSWER: The custom of allowing the women folk to make the first mistake has been projected from "real life" to the golf course. The gentleman should always bow his lady guest to the tee and then retreat to a point of vantage where he can watch her hips waggle. Many men have been known to yield the "honor" to a woman for the complete round, depending upon the contour of her posterior and the method by which she waggles.

QUESTION: Is a man supposed to retrieve a lady partner's tee?

ANSWER: This depends entirely upon the male. A man used to "picking up" around the house and the office will usually do the same on the golf course.

Pick-ups on the links often give a man a sense of satisfaction. Especially blondes.

DEPORTMENT ON THE FAIRWAY

QUESTION: What's the best way to play through a slow ladies' foursome?

ANSWER: Ancient custom demands that the approaching player simply cup his hand to his mouth and shout: "Fore!" This practice usually results in nothing more than a severe case of laryngitis, however, when used on the modern lady golfer.

Here are a few suggestions for handling those feminine sloths ahead:

(a) Have one of your group fall in a faint.

(b) Pick him up and carry him rapidly toward the foursome ahead. Explain that he has just had an attack

CADDY: A diminutive cad.

of Birdbath's Disease, and must be rushed to the hospital for surgery.

(c) This tactic will usually allow you to pass the ladies without questioning.

(d) Unless one of the dames happens to be a female surgeon.

(e) In which case, she might do the operation herself and delay your game.

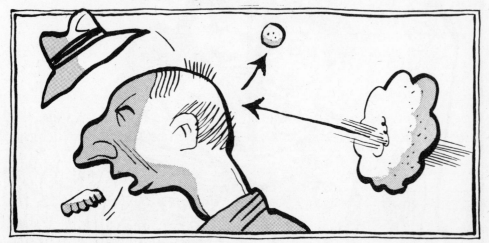

QUESTION: What's the proper thing to do when you hit a golfer up ahead?

ANSWER: Common courtesy demands that you offer some assistance to the unfortunate on the grass.

In case of head wounds, a simple packing can be made from a clean handkerchief.

For minor abrasions, lumps and bumps, cold water will ease the pain.

If patient is in a coma, start running for the doctor in the clubhouse.

If patient does not revive in ten minutes, start running for your lawyer.

QUESTION: What should I do after accidentally hitting another golfer's ball 200 yards up on the green?

ANSWER: Quickly throw him another new ball from your bag. You may never hit another shot like that for the rest of your life, you fool, you!

DEPORTMENT IN THE ROUGH

QUESTION: When my partner loses a golf ball, should I help him find it, or wait for him on the fairway?

ANSWER: The answer to this question depends entirely upon your opinion of your partner. If he is straightforward, upright and honest, let him find his own ball. If he happens to be straightforward, upright and a congenital liar, by all means watch him like a hawk.

QUESTION: Every time I hit into the rough, my partner follows me and laughs at me. What can I do to stop him?

ANSWER: Try a niblick, with closed stance; a long backswing and a smooth follow-through to the base of his skull.

DEPORTMENT ON THE GREEN

QUESTION: I find I can't putt when people watch me. How can I remedy this difficulty.

ANSWER: You are suffering from a severe case of anxiety neurosis, coupled with inhibited mother yearnings. The only way to cure your mania is through the cooperation of your golfing friends. When you reach the green, ask them to turn their backs and allow you to putt out. If they agree, simply putt out. If they refuse, try to convince them that you've finished lying about the game. If all else fails, play by yourself. Then you can lie to your heart's content.

23

QUESTION: What's the right time for conceding a putt to a competitor?
ANSWER: This is a truly difficult question. The National Golfing Rules and Lawn Seed Association tried to solve the problem only last year. They proclaimed every July 19th as National Conceded Putt Day throughout the land. The resulting statistics showed, however, that out of 1,987,654 putts close to the pin, only 17 were conceded.

The proper moments for conceding putts are as follows:

(1) When your opponent admits defeat and is willing to pay off.
(2) When your opponent is two inches from the cup and two down.
(3) When your opponent is ten feet from the cup — but happens to be your boss.
(4) Immediately after you've made a hole-in-one.

DEPORTMENT IN THE LOCKER ROOM

There are no rules for this situation.

Type Number One:

THE PERPETUAL TWITCH

This type of golfer appears to be afflicted with a combination of St. Vitus Dance and controlled epilepsy. He can be spotted immediately by the way he approaches the ball, a series of gestures and bodily contortions resembling a suspicious crab about to investigate a dangerous enemy.

Once established in a suitable position for striking the ball, the Twitch hesitates, arbitrates, meditates and then circumnavigates the area until satisfied that there are no loose atomic bombs under his feet. This maneuver may take anywhere from five minutes to an hour, depending upon the patience of his partners.

Once ready to smite the pill, the Twitch goes through a series of bodily contortions requiring full use of all the muscles controlling his posterior. Having started his motor running, he continues to bounce his hips, flex his shanks and vibrate his navel until every pore in his skin is bursting with dew.

After which, the damned fool usually tops the ball, anyhow.

Type Number Two:

THE RULE BOOK ROBOT

This unfortunate character approaches each fresh season with a headfull of expert advice gleaned from a long winter's perusal of the latest instruction books. In his mind's eye, he fancies himself a combination of Bobby Jones, Sammy Snead, Ben Hogan and Babe Zaharias, whose technique and mannerisms he plans to ape. The effort to imitate his idols, however, makes him look like nothing more graceful than a cigar store Indian aprowl on the fairways.

The Rule Book Robot fancies himself something of a sage at giving advice to others, and will quote his authorities chapter and verse when questioned by resentful friends and enemies. He is especially quick to criticize any golfer who manages to hit the ball a reasonable poke without slice or hook.

At the season's end, the average Rule Book Robot has abandoned his literary learning and may be discovered grumbling and groaning in the deep woods.

But when winter comes again, you'll find him back in his library boning up with a batch of fresh experts who will make him twice as funny looking next spring.

Type Number Three:

THE NERVELESS WONDER

This relaxed individual has practiced for years to achieve an indestructible calm. He seems equipped with iced blood, perpetual *savoir-faire,* and the nonchalance of a Casanova in milady's boudoir. He is an old hand in the game and has invented many cute and prosy sentiments to fit sudden emergencies.

When deep in the rough and hacking his way out, he will say: "Don't wait for me, boys, I'm drilling for oil."

When two down on the green, he will breathe: "Oh, well — what the hell — it's only a game, fellows."

After a horrible hook off the tee, he will remark: "I'm off again — on my own hook."

These quaint asides invariably endear him to his friends, who forever marvel at his quiet good humor, his even temper and his enviable philosophy. After a horrible day on the links, The Nerveless Wonder joins his mates in the locker room, buys a few rounds of drinks, engages in jokes, jibes and other lighthearted amusements. His actions are calculated to convince everybody that the high score he shot means nothing to him.

After which, he returns home, smites his wife with the mashie, kicks his children and beats his dog.

Type Number Four:

THE MUSCLE MAN

This bruising behemoth began his nefarious career in high school and college when he became a member of: the Football Team, the Wrestling Team, the Basketball Team, the Boxing Team, the Weight-lifting Team and the Swimming Team. He approaches the tee with a swagger, pausing long enough to allow any ladies in the audience to observe his sinewy bumps. After which, he lashes out at the ball in the manner of an axe-murderer.

The Muscle Man is convinced that golf is a game requiring great strength, and will laugh down his nose at any suggestion that he ease up on his backswing. He lifts the club as he would a baseball bat. He grits his teeth, closes his eyes and whips out at the pill so that every sinew in his body comes into play. The resulting breeze usually nets him:

(a) A sensationally long drive,

(b) A sensationally sharp slice, and

(c) A sensationally remote lie somewhere on the next fairway.

Type Number Five:

THE OLD PRO

This ancient party may be found on any golf course in the land, quietly hitting the little white ball straight down the fairway while his younger competitors sweat and swear in the woods. He dresses in a vague and rumpled style, generally giving the impression of an itinerant rag-picker on the prowl for stray debris. He is wizened and wrinkled and looks old enough to have played the game with Mary, Queen of Scots.

This fantasy ends abruptly when the Old Pro steps up to the tee. With nary a twitch or a wiggle, he brings his arthritic arms back in a creaking swing, follows through like an unoiled gate, and clobbers the ball for an easy two hundred and fifty yards. His younger adversaries, amused by the ancient boy's luck, snicker behind his back — and wait for him to collapse.

They are still waiting, when the Old Pro holes out on the 18th, smiling his sly smile, carding a low score, and collecting a small fortune in wagers from the group.

CONCENTRATE!

Alwayse keep thy heade dowyn — swinge deftly —
walke slowlye — and stryke while thy irone is hotte.
Ancient Scotch Proverb

The experts all agree that golf is a game compounded of nine-tenths ability and one-tenth damned fool luck. The element of chance exists for obvious reasons. The average golf course contains a minimum of 543 trees, any one of which can ricochet a bad shot to within inches of the pin.

Other experts argue that modern man is poorly equipped to play the game. He lacks the power of intense concentration. Only a professional can concentrate on such items as (a) choice of clubs, (b) swing, (c) distance, (d) wind, and (e) carry.

36

The run-of-the-mill golfer tries in vain to hold the above elements strongly in the mirror of his mind. He fails, naturally.

A recent survey shows that the average golfer has the following items on his mind when stepping up to the ball:

(a) His greens fee.
(b) His club dues.
(c) The sexy doll in the twosome just ahead.
(d) The blonde playing with her.
(e) The possibility of joining them at the next hole.
(f) The proper approach to the girls.
(g) Where to take them to dinner.
(h) Cost of same.
(i) Where to take them after dinner.
(j) Excuses to give wife for staying out late.
(k) Tomorrow's hangover.

cheep!

Concentration has been a stumbling block for the average player ever since the game was invented. He listens to a broad assortment of suggestions from the experts and tries one system after the other:

"Always keep your eye on the ball and your mind on the club," suggests Sammy Snide, last year's Florida Mixed High Ball Bourbon Champion.

"Head down, feet apart, hips straight, eyes front, back stiff, grip firm, knees in, ankles out, nostrils flared," cautions Ben Brogan, National Match Box Playoff Champion.

"In order to concentrate," advises a famous lady golfer, "I try to

AN IMPOSSIBLE LIE: Absolutely unplayable.

block out any stray thoughts in my brain, except the new middy-blouse I'm making. Pretty soon, I'm mentally sewing the buttons on the bodice. Since the buttons are round, they force me to think of other round objects. I work my way from buttons to oranges to flying saucers to meat balls. From here on in, it's a short jump from a meat ball to a golf ball. All I do is change the color, take off the ketchup and paint the meat ball white. Now it looks exactly like a golf ball. The next step is easy. I simply swing at the disguised meat ball on the tee. Anybody can do it. Especially players who like spaghetti and meat balls."

Lots of golfers are affected by extraneous noises, while preparing to swing at the ball. This lack of concentration is apt to cause serious loss of distance and should be remedied at once. Sometimes a nearby sound, though insignificant to others, may convert a normal player into a hopeless neurotic while on the links. Many golfers have been known to collapse upon hearing such noises as (a) a soft belch, (b) a discreet and muffled sneeze, (c) the chirp of a thrush in the brush, (d) the galloping of an ant on a plant, or (e) the commotion caused by anybody inhaling a cigarette in the immediate area.

The cure for such lack of concentration is obvious. The troubled player should immediately equip himself with a pair of extra-heavy ear muffs. These will cut out all noises within five feet of his ball. The use of such an outfit, however, might alienate him from his friends, who may consider him a hopeless psychotic. Such treatment is all to the good. By being forced to practice by himself, the plagued player can cut his score by at least twenty strokes, since there'll be nobody around to check up on his lies.

How to cure persistent loose-mindedness?

Any psychiatrist will tell you that you can't employ your mind to the fullest when you drag minor problems to the first tee. Step up to the ball with an optimistic attitude at all times. Think of something pleasant.

Think of a beautiful woman.

Imagine that she's the shapeliest, loveliest, most luscious gal in the whole world.

Put her on a boat, and get aboard with her.

Now wreck the boat on a desert island.

Ply her with cocoanuts.

Do not falter when she seizes you in her arms and kisses you madly. Return her affection.

As the moon rises over the tundra, mumble sweet nothings into her ear until she is breathless with emotion.

Then — as your lips meet hers — *swing out at that golf ball!*

What difference does it make if you missed?

You can go back and kiss her again on the next shot, can't you?

QUESTIONS AND ANSWERS ABOUT CONCENTRATION

QUESTION: I keep thinking of business problems when I'm playing golf. How can I learn to forget them?

ANSWER: Go into bankruptcy at once. This will permanently eliminate all office worries and cannot but help improve your game.

QUESTION: My name is Luella J. Leadbottom and I'm thirty-four years old, married, and a resident of South Goody's Nook, Iowa, where I'm a member of the Wednesday Afternoon Golfing Club at the Southside Cuff Links along with Janette Foldingpin, Marge Mummifier and Greta Grinniwig, all good friends of mine, but they seem to be affecting my game because every time we get started at the first tee the girls are always in the middle of a discussion about any number of things, like: styles, hats, lipsticks, bargain sales, what to cook for dinner, reducing diets, the high cost of living, and stuff like that, which makes it kind of difficult to concentrate on the ball when I step up to swing at it, when my mind is busy with thinking about what I was just talking about with the girls, so that I either miss the ball completely, or top it, or slice or hook it into the woods, after which I feel that maybe I've done something wrong and it could be that my mind was thinking of too many unimportant things and that was why I missed the ball, which is quite a problem to me and what can I do to eliminate it?

ANSWER: Shut up. You talk too much.

QUESTION: What can I do to help concentrate on the ball when I hit it? I can't seem to keep my head down.

ANSWER: It's very important that you watch the ball as you start your swing. Here's a method that's guaranteed to produce results:

(a) Go at once to your neighborhood jeweler.

(b) Purchase a diamond bracelet worth at least $10,000.00.

41

(c) Before each tee shot, lay the bracelet alongside the ball.

(d) Now swing. You'll find that nothing short of an atomic blast will force you to look away from the diamonds for fear somebody will steal them.

(e) Don't worry about hitting the bracelet. Genuine diamonds cannot be smashed by a golf stroke. If diamonds fall apart and disintegrate, return them to the jeweler for a refund.

(f) If jeweler refuses to refund your money, sue him.

CADDIES I HAVE KNOWN

Number One: THE FREE LESSON EXPERT

Every course, whether public or private, has at least a few of this type of caddy. He ranges in age from ten to sixty and usually makes his presence felt immediately. When you're addressing the ball, he will be heard to emit sly, clucking noises, somewhere between "Tssssk! Tssssk!" and "Good Heavens!" After which, with no encouragement at all, he will proceed to correct your stance, sneer at your backswing, chortle at your chip shots, and splutter at your putting.

By the time you reach the first green, he will have given you at least fifteen lessons in golf. At this point, you can get rid of him by any one of the following methods:

1. Offer him a bonus for keeping his trap shut.
2. Pay him off and send him back to the clubhouse.
3. Break a club over his head.

Number Two: THE HONEST STATISTICIAN

This type of caddy is usually young enough to be scrupulously honest and straightforward. To make things worse, the lad is majoring in high-school mathematics and is excessively proud of his ability to add figures in his head. This talent stands him in good stead whenever you ask him how many strokes you had on the previous hole. His adding machine brain makes a liar out of you every time.

A dramatic playlet, written after strangling the last youth of this type I used, goes something like this:

ME: (*Thinking deeply*) "Let's see now. The way I figure it, I took a five on that last hole."

CADDY: (*Examining a daisy*) "You did?"

Typical caddy giving instructions to masculine duffer.

Same caddy giving instructions to female duffer.

ME: "Didn't I?"

CADDY: "If you say so, sir."

ME: "I said so. I said I took a five."

CADDY: (*Whistling a popular air: "Mr. Five by Five"*) "You're the boss, sir."

ME: "Are you insinuating I'm a liar? Let's just review the hole, wise guy. My first shot took me into the woods. Then I came out with a five iron —"

CADDY: "Out? Your five iron shot hit a rock, sir. Then it ricocheted into that sandpit, remember?"

ME: (*Sheepishly*) "My mistake. I was three down in the sandpit. Then I came out with my eight iron and —"

CADDY: "Out? Your eight iron shot hit the oak tree on the fairway, sir, after which it lodged in a finch's nest. You hit the nest up into the tree, whereupon the bird settled on the golf ball, thinking it was an egg. You dropped another ball and aimed for the green."

ME: (*Meekly*) "Hahahahahaha — so I did. Funny thing, my forgetting about that bird. Well, well. Of course. That put me in the sand trap near the green in eight strokes —"

CADDY: "Not quite, sir. Your eighth shot, if you will recall, hooked into the big pond near the hunting preserve. The ball was grabbed by a duck floating by. The duck took flight and headed south, but before it could gain altitude a hidden hunter shot it down from the canebrake. Since the ball was in the duck, it became the hunter's possession legally, he said. You disagreed and we took the case to court, where it was tried before Judge Oscar Calumny of the Tenth District. The judge ruled against you and fined you fifty dollars for illegally feeding golf balls to ducks. His verdict killed your case and put us back on the fairway in ten strokes, since the ball was lost in the duck. After that, you overshot the green with your spoon, came out of the weeds with your niblick and four-putted the cup to make your total for the hole exactly sixteen strokes."

ME: (*Slyly*) "You're wrong, sonny. You've left out one stroke."

CADDY: "I did? Which one was that?"

ME: (*Violently*) "This one!"

(*Whereupon I commenced to clobber the unfortunate youth
into insensibility, using my Number Seven iron in a short
backswing until he lay stiff and quiet on the greensward.*)

Number Three: OLD GRAND-DAD

Every golf course on earth owns at least one character of this type,
affectionately called "Pop," "Dad," or "The Old Man" by his brother
caddies. Though resembling a tottering corpse in his superstructure,
this wizened bag of bones shows no strain on the long hills and can
follow the spoor of a missing golf ball through countless miles of un-
charted veldt.

When encouraged by a kind word, the reasons for his impossible
strength are yours for the asking. An authentic history of one of these

muscular cadavers became mine when I interviewed a typical sample at the Creeping Crepuscle Links, in Upper Platte. Saskatchewan:

"My name," he told me, "is Typical J. Sample. I was born in the backroom of the last century, of poor but proud parents. When I was three, my father hit me with a badly sliced golf ball. From then on, my fate was sealed. I began to caddy for the local gentry long before puberty; and worked my way into the professional class by dint of hard work, strong arms, and a keen flair for spotting balls among the hibiscus. I am now married, have a wife, seven children and dog named Samuel Snead. I like caddying because it keeps me out in the air, on my toes, and in the pink. My hobbies are: posy sniffing, weaving anti-maccassars, and Arthur Godfrey. Who can ask for anything more?"

When pressed for further small talk, this old buzzard will quickly tell you that he has caddied for: Bobby Jones, Babe Didrickson, Patty Berg, Tommy Armour, The Marx Brothers, Ike Eisenhower, Mahatma Gandhi and the Swami of Cackowatt. This will inevitably lead him to making glib comments about your method of swinging at the ball, comparing your stroke favorably with those of such players as Gene Sarazen, Whiffy Cox and Ben Hogan.

This will inevitably cost you plenty when you pay him off.

"Never forget that Gene Sarazen," the old man will remind you. "Gave me a fifteen dollar tip on nine holes. Come to think of it, son, you look a lot like him — especially around the face."

See what I mean?

THE LADIES

Number One:

SEXY SUZIE

Here's a little known morsel of statistics, unexplored by Doctor Kinsey, probably because he didn't send his investigators into the links. The records show that one out of every ten females plays the game to gather wolf whistles, oglings and other masculine manifestations of admiration.

The drawing on the opposite page illustrates a compilation of scientific facts concerning the Sexy Suzie type of lady golfer. She is usually of average size and built generously both fore and aft. Suzie invariably appears at the first tee attired in a sweater that makes Marilyn Monroe resemble Orphan Annie. Her skirt is designed of a simple tweed of giant squares colored red, yellow, magenta and old puce. Her hair is combed loose, in the manner of a Hollywood siren rigged for a bedroom scene.

Having powdered her nose, lacquered her lips and varnished her eyebrows, Sexy Suzie leaves the clubhouse, walking slowly but with a gently swaying movement. By this time, every available male in the clubhouse has rushed avidly to the tee, where the entire group takes up a position five degrees off her starboard beam.

Having drawn her audience, Suzie now proceeds to address the ball in the manner of a burlesque queen with ants in her stance. After which she marches down the fairway, followed by a masculine foursome destined to play lousy golf behind her. After all, a diligent golfer must keep his eye on the ball!

50

Number Two:

THE LADY LEECH

This feminine finch is always spotted in the company of her unfortunate husband, a small and tired little man who looks as happy as a murderer on his way to the lethal chamber. Years ago, in a weak moment, he invited his little chicadee to come out and play the game with him. Ever since that black day she has joined him in every activity including fishing, hunting, bowling, badminton, parcheesi and deep breathing.

"Harry and I do everything together," she will explain, while Harry nods meekly, wondering whether he can lose her for a long enough time to visit the locker room on his own.

Her presence at Harry's side, however, rarely helps his game. He finds himself deliberately hitting the ball out of bounds, so that he can grab himself a few happy moments away from her.

This type of male rarely becomes a decent golfer, since he is always boiling with an internal rage and finds himself quaking and shivering whenever he handles a golf club. Psychiatrists claim that such repressions carry a man into the world of fantasy where he schemes strange pastimes with his mashie.

Like breaking it over her head, for instance.

Number Three:

THE YAKKETY FOURSOME

This covey of quaint quail can be spotted on any golf course and is usually found with a group of moaning males directly behind it. The ladies play a slow and studious game and will pause at the drop of an adjective to engage in conversation on any subject pleasant to the group. The quartet is composed of:

(a) A housewife, who will talk freely on: babies, dishes, meals, husbands, washing machines, diapers and sex.

(b) A single lady, who will talk freely on: men, books, the habits of mice, lice and rice.

(c) A school teacher, who will discuss: schools, rules, fools, tools and stools.

(d) An aged spinster, who will offer a few words on: flowers, birds, bees, beasts, weather, heather and leather.

It is estimated that an average group of this sort will bandy no less than 456,980 words about during a normal eighteen hole game. This sort of badinage irritates the male foursome behind them, who cannot seem able to break through the sound barrier, since all four ladies appear to be suffering from faulty hearing.

The resulting situation forces the pursuing males to use odd bird calls, hoots, hollerings and yowls.

Usually followed by small, crisp, four letter words.

Number Four:

HIGH-STYLE HATTIE

Why do women play golf?

A significant poll, taken by The Significant Poll Company last Whitsuntide, reveals the following amazing facts:

49% of all lady golfers play the game to escape the drudgery of house work.

23% of the girls roam the links in search of mates.

19% of the wrens join golf clubs to play Canasta.

8% of the ladies take up the sport to keep tabs on their husbands.

1% of the girls play the game because they like golf.

Further research into the habits of the females revealed that 6 out of every 10 women engage in the sport because of the yen for new fashions. The other 4 women in 10 play the game simply to find out what the original 6 are wearing. This may be confusing to masculine golfers, but should be crystal clear to the lady players.

The drawing on the opposite page shows what happens when an internationally famous designer gets his hooks into golfing apparel. The costume was created by Chrispin Fott, and shows a decidedly Spanish influence, since the outfit was sewed and stitched for wives of matadors playing the Grandeedee Links in Old Granada. Chrispin Fott believes that the tight toreador pants should allow the girls more freedom of movement, especially if any stray bulls happen to be browsing along the fairways.

Number Five:

FANNY FRUMP

This pudgy, unattractive lass looks out of place in any gathering of femininity on the golf course. Fanny Frump appears at the first tee dressed in a sweater designed out of an old flour sack, complete with natural pleats on the buskin. Her hat resembles a flagellated flapjack, and her skirt looks like something the family dog slept on.

Fanny's face sports no lipstick, rouge or powder, and her hair hangs in disordered strands and hunks, blown and tossed by every fitful breeze. All in all, this unfortunate woman would look better behind a plug horse, gathering rags and old papers on your village street.

Yet, despite Fanny's repulsive figure, despite her corrugated stockings and ulcerated shoes, she is sought out by every other woman in the club as a golfing partner.

Can you blame them?

Fanny invariably shoots in the low seventies!

EXTRA! EXTRA!
GOLFER'S MENTAL CLOSET
LAID OPEN!

The golfing kingdom was recently sent into spasms of shivers and shakes by Professor J. Edgar Kinsigh, the famous researcher. Kinsigh has already surveyed the sexual behavior of men, girls, lads, rodents, lemmings, and minor molluscs, but his findings on the *homus golfus* bid fair to put his other scientific findings into the laboratory ashcan.

"To begin with," said Kinsigh, when pressed for the hot news, "I knew that my first job meant finding a golfer we could call average. This was not easy; but after four years, we finally located our specimen. His name was Silas V. Average and he hailed from Taxi, Vermont. He stood five feet two, had eyes of blue, two petal pink ears, and a nose which hung down vertically from between his optics. He was mar-

61

ried, had a wife, two kids, a car, a dog, a mortgage and a bad cough from smoking too many cigarettes. He suffered from the usual domestic diseases, such as headaches, post-nasal drip, and bad stomach pains after eating fried foods. An intensive study of his brain while standing at the tee revealed the following goings-on in his mental chambers:

Section "A": THE SEX LOBE

This X-ray diagram of the patient's brain shows what happens when he sees a pretty girl ahead of him. Notice how the image in the lobe has been divested of normal attire. Notice, too, that the image is waving at him. This gesture will invariably cause the damned fool to wave back mentally. When this happens, all of his mental energy will flow out toward the pretty item on his mind, causing immediate hot and cold running flushes, sweating along the lower metatarsal, and a very bad swipe at the golf ball.

Section "B": THE CONSCIENCE LOBE

This smaller area of the brain is reserved for routine responsibilities such as the picture of his wife, as shown in the drawing. When this lobe is left open immediately following random thoughts of other women, a severe traumatic shock takes place, causing strong muscular quiverings, dry throat, spots before the eyes, and eventual topping of the golf ball.

Section "C": THE OFFICE LOBE

Here we find another area of the brain devoted to the player's deeper worries. Notice that the boss has appeared to bawl out the golfer for going around with other women. This may lead to further loss of distance at the tee and the possibility of loss of job at the office.

Section "D": THE MONEY LOBE

This department of the cranium is always a jumbled mess of figures and calculations concerned with: (a) the high cost of living, (b) the dues unpaid at the club, (c) the balance in the bank, and (d) how much it may cost to entertain the dame who's still hanging around Section "A."

Section "E": THE BALL LOBE

This tiny part of the brain is reserved for the golf ball itself. Notice how the ball seems to be laying in a vague, misted area. This means that the player has sliced it into the woods and can't possibly find it.

TRYING TO MAKE PAR: Playing around in the low seventies.

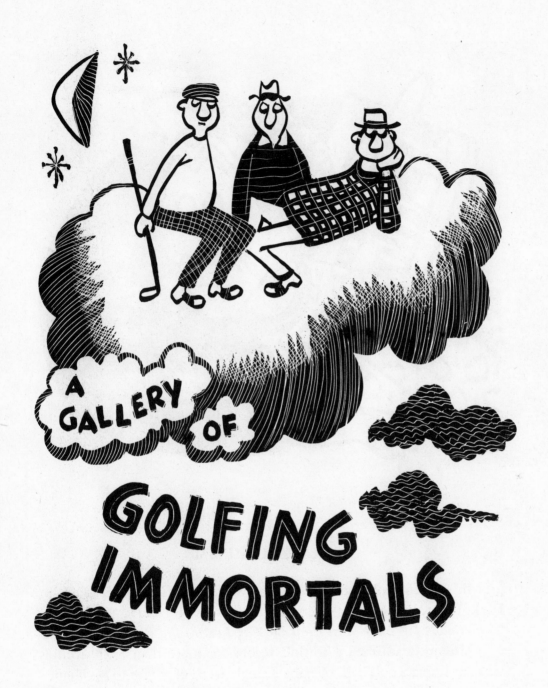

A GALLERY OF GOLFING IMMORTALS

HORACE K. MUMM

In a recent poll conducted at the Sleeping Crumb Golf Club, in Dark Closet, Idaho, the membership voted Horace K. Mumm as *"The Caddy I Would Most Prefer to Get Lost in the Woods With."*

Mumm established a world's record for more than 5,000 rounds without losing a golf ball, offering a single word of advice to his clients, or suggesting any corrections in the scoring. In addition to these accomplishments, Mumm has never been known to cough, belch or sneeze while a player teed off. At the end of each round, whether the tip offered him was a dime or a dollar, Mumm simply tipped his hat and said: "Thank you, sir."

REGINALD FESTLETHUMB

Reginald looms high on the list of outstanding personalities at the Old Sandpit Links, in Outer Overcoat, Minn. He established a new world's record last week when the club gave him the following citation:

"Be it known to all that Reginald Festlethumb has been a member of Old Sandpit for more than fifteen years. During this period, Reginald has entered the locker room a total of 52,876 times. Not once in Festlethumb's 52,876 visits was he ever heard to tell a single joke involving either a Traveling Salesman, a Farmer, or a Farmer's Daughter."

LESTER FOLDINGBURST

Lester is the club pro at the Falling Arch Links, in South Phlegm, N. J. He broke into prominence last summer because of his treatment of a pupil named Arthur Chumpington, the millionaire bank president.

Lester was overheard to tell Chumpington the following:

"Listen, chump, you're paying me twenty bucks an hour for nothing. You swing like a corroded gate. You're as blind as a bat. Your stance is best suited for steering a pushcart. You'll never learn to play the game. Give it up and try quoits."

GENEVIEVE Z. THROOP

Genevieve's claim to fame comes about because of her distinctive personality. Her husband, Haskell Throop, has been an avid golfer for the past thirty years. Yet, Genevieve allows him to play any time he chooses, loves to see him in the great outdoors, and has never been known to bawl him out when he returns late for dinner.

"Why should I scold him?" inquires Genevieve. "It's wonderful to know exactly where he is when he leaves me home alone. He's got his rights. But so have I. I entertain my boy friends whenever Haskell plays golf."

ARBUTHNOT Q. FULLBIRD

Arbuthnot distinguished himself at the Elbow Rub Course in the spring of last year by shooting a hole in one on the 345 yard (Par 4) water hole.

Arbuthnot neither swooned nor shouted, and to this day has spoken not one word of his prowess into any listening ear.

The fact that Arbuthnot is a deaf mute may have something to do with this phenomenon.

SAMSON P. BURLAP

Top honors for distinguished golfing go to Samson this year, as a reward for outstanding behavior in the face of insurmountable odds. Burlap, when one down in the tall grass, emerged hours later — and made the following statement after holing out:

"Fact is, I got caught in a gopher hole back there and it took a lot of digging to knock the pill out of the grass. I finally dislodged it after rooting more than two feet under the dirt. I'll take a 58 for the hole, boys."

HOW TO STAND ON YOUR OWN TWO FEET

Do you use your feet correctly at the tee?
Is your weight on your right shoe?
Do you stand on your toes?
Are you a roundheel?
Are your feet firmly planted?
What about six-toed golfers?

These are only a few of the many questions that distress the beginner at the tee. He prepares to smite the ball in a state of mental turmoil simply because he has suddenly discovered that he knows nothing about his feet. The fact that a normal man can walk, run, hop, jump, skip and trip means little when addressing the ball. The neophyte stands gawking at the tee, sweating in all pores while he shakes his posterior, wiggles his ears, waggles his hips, knocks his knees and hops about from one foot to another like a small boy caught too far from the backhouse.

To avoid such gymnastics, it's absolutely necessary to learn the proper address. Your pro will tell you that perfect balance is the most important single factor needed for the correct swing. In golf, as in love, effective stroking can only take place when you have assumed a comfortable stance.

THE SQUARE STANCE

This position requires placing both feet the same distance from an imaginary line parallel to the line of flight. (To determine the line of flight, simply measure the distance from the tee to the green. Now divide by twenty. This will give you the approximate distance your ball will travel. For longer holes, use longer tape measures.)

THE CLOSED STANCE

To achieve the closed stance, simply pull your right foot back from the imaginary line, in the same way you jerk that foot for doing the rhumba. Next, adjust hips so that you feel no strain on the ilium. (To determine location of your ilium, simply measure the distance from your knee to your neck. Now detour at the navel, making a sharp turn over the hip bone. For large and cumbersome hip bones, consult your doctor.)

THE OPEN STANCE

Same as above, but substitute your left foot for your right foot.

THE HAPPENSTANCE

By far the most popular of all postures, this system is used by over 90 per cent of all beginners. It requires no rules at all, other than the general confusion resulting from too much instruction. Simply spread the legs and bend the knee that suits your fancy. It doesn't matter whether you concentrate or not. You'll top the shot, anyhow.

A FEW HINTS AND TIPS

In order to place yourself for the shot, make sure the bottom of the club sits evenly on the turf.

If the toe of your club sticks up off the ground, you are too far away. Sneak up closer, watching the club head as it settles down. If club heel goes up, you have come too far and must retreat again. Walk slowly backward and forward until the proper adjustment is made, then relax for a moment before making your next move. When foursome behind you shouts "Fore!" at you impatiently, lift your head in their direction and shout back: "Drop dead!"

This may force you to begin your stance all over again. Take your time. Even when they begin to shoot golf balls over your head.

When you've learned the perfect stance, your arms should hang straight down from your shoulders. For players whose arms hang on the bias, a few trips to your neighborhood chiropractor should prove profitable.

Especially for the chiropractor.

The experts say that the distance between your feet should be approximately equivalent to the width of your shoulders. This rule, however, does not apply to sports who wear padded jackets.

QUESTIONS AND ANSWERS ABOUT YOUR STANCE

QUESTION: I happen to be pigeon-toed. How on earth can I take the right stance?

ANSWER:　Play with pigeons exclusively.

QUESTION: Is it possible to hit the ball well with flat feet?

ANSWER:　Never. Always use a golf club.

QUESTION: Which do I take first, the grip, or the stance?

ANSWER:　This is difficult to establish, since players differ so much temperamentally. For golfers who twitch and tremble at the tee, the stance should come first, since excessive writhing and squirming will often shake the club out of the player's hand. Give yourself a full three minutes of fidgeting and jerking at the tee.

If shivers do not cease, allow the next foursome to play through while you swallow a small dose of nembutal. This sedative is certain to stop all muscular twitching. It will also put you to sleep.

QUESTION: Is it all right for me to spread my legs so far apart?

ANSWER: *Pullease, lady!*

BUYING EQUIPMENT CAN
BE FUN?

The poor workman always blames his tool.
Memoirs of Casanova

Whilst browsing through my five-foot shelf of bits and morsels concerning the greatest game on earth, I came across the following definition:

GOLF: *A game of Dutch origin which consists in driving with an implement, called a club, a hard, gutta percha ball from a tee to a hole in the ground, anywhere from 150 to 500 yards distant.*

This definition, although probably comprehensible to the ancient

GOLFING BAG: The female partner you always draw in a mixed foursome.

Dutch burghers, is pretty damned foolish to any modern sportsman interested in the game. In the old days, golf was limited to the upper strata of society. Only an Earl, Duke or Lord could manage to afford the time, the expense and the general confusion involved in the pastime. The common man, bound to his menial chores, had little chance to do anything more than stand on the sidelines and sneer at the ridiculous vices of his peers.

Today, however, things have changed. Everybody knows that millions of golf balls are being pounded into the deep woods by a weird assortment of enthusiasts, all of whom burn with the yen to hack at least twenty strokes from their scores. This national frustration has created a merchandising market that yields buckets of loot to the American business man.

The advertising gentry, entranced by so broad a sucker group for dry goods and sundries, retired to their Madison Avenue idea foundries and didn't emerge until every angle of the game was covered with ample snares and traps for the golfer's hard-earned buck. A quick romp through the advertising pages of a magazine yielded the following sample of the huckster's art:

BLAST OFF WITH THE ROCKET BALL!

Having trouble with your tee shots?

Tired of averaging only 46 yards with your driver?

Disgusted with your slices, hooks and chips?

Are you fumbling your club?

Do you blush, stammer and flinch when addressing the ball?

Eliminate all these mental woes! The ROCKET BALL is guaranteed to carry over 800 yards — or your money back!

The ROCKET BALL was designed and invented by the scientist who developed the atom bomb. The moment your club head strikes the ball a chain reaction of atomic energy is set off. WHAM! BAM! WHOOSH! You'll be delighted with the new power in your stroke.

IF YOU'RE MISSIN'—TRY ATOMIC FISSION!

Read what Herkimer J. Perkimer of Bent Elbow, Nebraska, says:

"I used to be all thumbs and toes when I stepped up to the first tee. Then I bought a ROCKET BALL. My first shot sailed for over a half mile — and I haven't found it yet. Please send searching party at once. I am lost."

Statistics show that there are over fifty brands of golf balls being manufactured today. This means that more than fifty advertising agencies are employing creative prose pests to discover new qualities for their merchandise. The result of such mental madness has blessed the humble golf ball with the following entrancing characteristics. Today, balls are guaranteed to:

    (a) Travel greater distances.
    (b) Correct a golfer's slice.
    (c) Correct a golfer's hook.
    (d) Correct a golfer's lack of confidence.
    (e) Correct a golfer's bad temper.
    (f) Correct the pro's bank balance.

It's about time somebody put an end to such obvious deceit. Any fool knows that a golf ball is equipped only to:

    (1) Bounce.
    (2) Roll.
    (3) Get lost.

Any golfer worthy of his salt knows that he must buy a few golf balls before he can play the game. The beginner should walk, and not run, to the nearest sporting goods emporium and purchase five dozen of the first brand he sees. It doesn't matter whether the ball has special qualities.

You'll lose all of them at the first water hole, anyhow.

DRESSES

"Ladies' dresses" (according to Patty Berg, in her instruction book: *Golf Illustrated*) *"should be loose enough to permit complete freedom, but should fit well enough for comfort."*

This suggestion may be all right for Patty, but a consensus of female golfers, recently surveyed by the Female Golfers Consensus Company, reveals contradicting testimony. Most lassies prefer a minimum of looseness in the skirt, allowing only an inch of leeway for the preliminary waggling before the stroke. All other waggles after that become wiggles, calculated to attract the masculine optics in the four-some behind.

SHIRTS

Women who wear shirts are not ladies.

SWEATERS

The sweater is a "must" for all feminine golfers between the ages of 12 through 35. (After 35, it doesn't matter what a lady golfer wears.) Truly stylish women prefer sweaters of all types and varieties, all of which must be purchased at least three sizes too small. This makes for delightful warmth for the lady player and has the same effect on all observant males.

GLOVE

Men and women alike purchase a glove for the left hand. Experts say that it reduces calluses and aids in gripping the club, especially in sticky weather, hurricanes, monsoons, blizzards and cloudbursts. These reasons, of course, are utter nonsense. Golfers buy these fool gloves because they look professional and give players an air of experience and *savoir faire*.

You can get the same effect by having a stiff drink of Bourbon before each round.

HATS

Most good lady golfers go hatless. This may explain their proficiency at the game, since good lady golfers usually play with other ladies who are good lady golfers. The absence of hats cuts down the opportunity for small talk and fashion discussions. Women who want to improve their game should buy simple visors, tams, or hair nets. This will discourage stupid gossip in a female foursome.

Women who don't give a damn should try canasta.

CLUBS

Now we come to the most important equipment in the game, the sticks with which to flail at the air. The usual method of selection for beginners involves (a) the pro at the club, (b) the pro at the sporting equipment store, or (c) the amateur who can get it for you wholesale.

Of the three, Method C is used most often.

Probably the best means of choosing a club is by "feel." The amateur should test at least five dozen models of each club before laying his money down on the counter. This problem involves many visits to various stores, but the resolute shopper should not abandon his search, despite the blandishments of the sales help.

If a sporting goods salesman approaches you with: "Pardon, sir, can I help you?"

The sly customer should say at once: "No, thanks, I'm just feeling."

This simple statement will immediately tell the nosy salesman where you stand. If he persists in trying to make a sale, start swinging as if you were cutting grass. You may clip him on the shin. That should teach him a golf lesson.

Buying a golf club is really very simple. Just remember that you must guard against purchasing sticks that are:

    (a) Too heavy.
    (b) Too light.
    (c) Too "whippy."
    (d) Too long.
    (e) Too short.
    (f) Too heavy in the head, while light in the shaft.
    (g) Too light in the head, while heavy in the shaft.
    (h) Too whippy in the shaft, while heavy in the head.
    (i) Too expensive, while just right in the head and shaft.

The best procedure, of course, is to consult the nearest professional. He will always help you out by talking you into buying the set of clubs best suited for your weight, height and build. By dumping the responsibility squarely on his shoulders you will eliminate any personal guilt in the choice, and can always blame your bad shots on *"that dog of a pro who advised me to get these ***!!! clubs!"*

GOLF BAG

Most golfers consider their bags a mark of personal prestige and will usually go into hock to impress their friends on the links. This peculiar mental aberration is responsible for the modern assortment of golf luggage now being peddled in every sporting goods emporium in the land. The up-to-date golf bag is manufactured in King Size these days and comes in a variety of leathers, including: Pigskin, Calf, Cowhide, Alligator, Zebra and Old Mink.

The sensible male golfer can get along with any container rigged to carry a simple load of clubs. Even an old burlap bag has been known to do.

The sensible female golfer must provide, however, for a bag big enough to contain at least the following articles:

Full set of clubs
Small handbag
Powder puff and case
Lipstick
Rouge
Eyebrow pencil
Comb
Brush
Mirror
Hair net
Sweater
Box of Kleenex
Cold cream

Carton of cigarettes
Cigarette lighter
Lighter fuel
Box of flints
Parasol, in case of sunshine
Umbrella, in case of rain
Eyeglasses
Eyeglass cleaners
Sunglasses
Sunglass cleaners
Tees
Car keys

TEES

In ancient days the frugal Scotsman considered a small mound of sand an appropriate resting place for the golf ball. The Scotch sportsman moulded the sand with his fingers.

After which he proceeded to whack the hide off the ball for hundreds of yards down the fairway.

Modern science has labored long and hard to save the present day golfer such silly labor. The tee of today is fabricated of special woods and plastics, designed to afford a proper nest for the ball, and colored in bright and garish hues so that the golfer's eye can see it easily.

After which he proceeds to whack the hide off the ball — for approximately fifty yards into the rough.

MASCULINE DRESS

A masculine golfer should never wear a dress.

SHOES

While rummaging through the thousands of volumes needed as background research for this book, I came across a quaint little tome written by Babe Didrickson Zaharias: *Championship Golf.*

Babe says: *"Next to your clubs, shoes are the most important consideration in your equipment.... You cannot concentrate on your golf shots while worrying about your feet slipping and sliding."*

This advice, though probably appreciated by all women who slip and slide on a golf course, doesn't mean much to the average masculine golfer. Take the case of Leo Diegel, for instance, as quoted in *Swinging Into Golf* (Jones and Brown). Leo was able to rap out a neat score in the low 70's (for 18 holes!) while *standing on his right foot alone.*

This feat either proves that Leo Diegel just doesn't give a damn about his metatarsals, or that Babe Zaharias suffers from too much worry about her brogans.

The answer to the shoe problem is perfectly simple. Try to wear shoes when playing golf. The use of shoes eliminates getting splinters in your feet. Shoes are also a great boon to ticklish golfers, who often spoil good approach shots when standing on snakes and frogs.

For golfers who insist upon playing in their bare feet, there are certain clubs where no shoes are required. These establishments are usually connected with nudist camps where members don't wear anything else, either. Nudist golfers, however, rarely achieve low scores — too many distractions along the way.

QUESTIONS AND ANSWERS ABOUT EQUIPMENT:

QUESTION: Suppose I can't afford to buy a full set of four woods and ten irons, which clubs would you recommend?

ANSWER: Don't let your bank account discourage you from playing the game! Start with a short iron and a putter. Approach your nearest golf club just before dark. Sneak in and practice chip shots on one of the greens. If the watchman catches you, tell him you're out hunting snakes. Always carry a snake with you to prove your honesty. Make sure to use a full-grown rattler. When watchman sees the snake, he will be convinced you're an honest man. When snake lunges at the watchman, beat the reptile smartly across the head with your short iron. Use a smooth, grooved swing and make sure to follow through. Correct stroke should decapitate the snake. Incorrect stroke should hospitalize watchman, after which you can visit the course every night without worrying about him.

QUESTION: I've tried every type of club on the market, but still can't score under 200 for 18 holes. What shall I do?

ANSWER: Start taking lessons from the club Pro. You should have at least three hours of lessons each day. This will cost you about $210.00 per week. Continue the lessons for about eight months. The total cost will then be $6,720.00, an amount that will drive you into bankruptcy and force you to abandon the game — which is what you should have done in the first place.

QUESTION: My hands and wrists are very weak. What should I do?

ANSWER: This is a difficult question. Try squeezing tennis balls in your spare time to strengthen your hands. If you can't get tennis balls, try thumbing melons, clutching at straws, or strangling your wife. When you can strangle your wife easily, your wrists should be ready for swinging golf clubs. But are you? There are no golf links in San Quentin.

THE SHORT PUTT – AND
HOW TO GRAB IT

*A straight line is the shortest
distance between two putts . . .
Archimedes*

PURPLE HOLE, Wis., April 7, 1954. After many moons of patient search, investigation, exploration and field work, your correspondent was finally able to corner the most fascinating golfing character on earth: Lucius X. Slyme, the champion putt goniff extant. Slyme disappeared from the golfing world over a year ago after successfully stealing more than 10,976 conceded putts in less than five years of active play, a record that may stand forever as the ultimate in thievery on the green.

"My last game," confessed Slyme, "forced me into sudden retirement on the 18th hole of the Creeping Coma Golf Club. I managed to pick up my ball a distance of eight feet from the pin and walk off without a word from my opponents. The fact that they came after me with brandished clubs after they holed out explains my living in this cave ever since. I overstretched their credulity. They're waiting for me with drawn swords and howitzers, should I ever return to the game."·

When asked for a brief summary of his career, Slyme came forth with the following facts:

"Anybody with a bit of gumption and enough brass could do what I did," admitted Slyme. "I began my training as a mere youth, practicing my wiles during such childish games as checkers, parcheesi and blind-man's buff. These simple pastimes soon bored me and I advanced to the more intricate and adult sports involving greater risks and more confidence, games like poker, bridge, pinochle and canasta. Here I studied diligently until I was able to lay down a losing bridge hand four tricks short of the game and get away with it. My technique was simple. *'The rest of the tricks are mine,'* I would say confidently, spreading my cards quickly before my opponents and then sweeping the dummy toward me in one motion. When I had perfected the technique, I knew I was ready for golf."

When pressed for a breakdown of his tactics on the green, Slyme hedged and balked, hesitating to proffer his sage advice unless I conceded it was worth a stipulated amount of money for his efforts. I conceded, of course.

Here, in its complete form, is Slyme's completed manuscript concerning trickery at the pin:

1: ADOPTING THE CORRECT ATTITUDE

The most important asset for a putt thief is his "air," or attitude on the green. The neophyte must take great pains to establish himself as an expert at sinking any putt within two feet of the cup. Once your opponents realize that you can successfully drop almost every short putt, they will relax and allow you to steal the longer ones.

When this point is reached, you have arrived at the crucial test for your talents as a robber. Walk up to the green boldly, looking neither to the right or left. Pick up your ball and wave to the next man player casually. At this stage, many amateur thieves make the mistake of waiting for an approving nod from their competitors. This is bad procedure. Instead, merely reach for your score card and proceed to mark down your total for the hole.

Remember that a seasoned safecracker doesn't wait around to ask permission from his victim.

Walk, do not run, to the next tee.

2: WHAT TO DO WHEN CHALLENGED

Many beginning putt-grabbers are worried about the inevitable reaction from their mates in the foursome. To eliminate such concern, it's wise to practice "getting away with it" on outside personalities. For fortifying experience in the art, experiment by trying to talk your way out of the following predicaments.

(1) Come home late with lipstick on your cheek and blonde hairs on your lapel. Convince your wife all this is meaningless.

(2) Drive the wrong way up a one-way street. When cop arrives, try to worm out of it.

(3) Run for election as Mayor of your town. When elected, abscond with the town treasury. When caught, invent a suitable alibi. When jailed, practice your wiles on the jailors.

A GOOD BACKSWING: The hottest corner on the golf club porch.

EXTRA EQUIPMENT WAVE
TO HIT THE NATION!

INSIDE STORY OF GOLFING GONIFFS EXPOSED!

FLATBUSH, N. Y., May 12.— While innocent golfers wandered the nation's links this fine spring morning, few knew that a secret band of determined men were mulling the future of golf in a smoke-filled closet in Flatbush.

"We are mulling the future of golf in a smoke-filled closet in Flatbush," admitted Lester R. Mordant, "because we are a secret band of determined men."

This incriminating statement led our reporter to explore the premises in search of important evidence concerning the mysterious conclave. Determined sniffing close to the bar, the washroom and the juke box revealed odds and ends of commercial gossip destined to stagger every golfer worthy of his mashie. Manufacturers from every branch of business on earth had gathered to discuss new methods for raiding the wallets of the nation's sportsmen. After a solid week of small talk and planning, the sly tycoons slinked away into the night, leaving behind them a bevy of cigar butts, broken glasses, and pencil stubs.

The following notes and scrawlings were retrieved from a wastebasket by our reporter who happened to be wandering near the local dump. The message is clear. Those rascals have set their snares for any loose buck available. Before the next mistral blows across your favorite links, the sporting goods emporiums will be stacked high with a variety of useless merchandise calculated to make any redblooded golfer's blood pressure do nip-ups.

As a public service, our Department of Lumps and Slices has lumped all available hunks of evidence into readable warnings and submits them herewith as a shopper's guide. The reader is cautioned that the following diagrams and data were born, bred and buttered out of the memory of our reporter. Any similarity between the items pictured and future manufactured junk is purely coincidental and not intended to reflect the views of the publisher, his editors, or his relatives:

1: THE RAINY DAY ROUSTABOUT

Are you bothered when sudden squalls splat you on the links? Do monsoons, tornadoes, hurricanes and cloudbursts affect your game? Do you cringe and shrink when lightning cleaves a tree near you?

The Rainy Day Roustabout was perfected to solve all your weather problems, mates! Easy to install, the special collar (A) attaches easily to your neck and is guaranteed not to sully your epiglottis, or loosen your larynx. Simply turn the clamp, adjust the straps, and you are ready to play golf in *any weather!*

The umbrella itself (B) is made of sturdy cloth and comes equipped with a special lightning rod (C) which prevents any passing electrical bolt from distracting you.

The Rainy Day Roustabout can be bought in shades of old rose, puce, magenta and yellow ochre.

Our special price to you................................ $87.97

2: THE SAND TRAP SCOPE

This masterpiece of engineering was designed to help even the worst duffer out of sand traps. Specially constructed for the deep (or ravine type) traps, the handy Sand Trap Scope is guaranteed to afford the player a glimpse of fresh air on the green above. Nobody likes to keep slamming at the ball without knowing *where* he's going. With

The Sand Trap Scope, you can gain altitude, direction, optimism and even hope. No other periscope can make *that* claim.

Golfer Samuel Snide says: *"The Sand Trap Scope is simply peachy. Makes landing in deep traps a pleasure. Especially if you're playing behind gals like Marilyn Monroe."*

Priced for quick clearance.............................. $8.75

4: DEADPAN MASK

Are you frightened and jittery in competitive play? Do you twitch, itch, bounce and jounce whenever you're in a money game? Does the sight of a two-foot putt make your blood-pressure rise? Do you bite your lip? Chew your gums? See blots before your eyes?

The Deadpan Mask was designed for all players who go to pieces under pressure. Made of flesh-colored plastic, it will fit neatly over your twitching pan so that even your wife won't recognize you. Simply put it on when the score gets tight, and bang that ball into the hole.

"My friends used to laugh when I approached the tee in a money game," says Horace M. Barrass. *"Now I don't care what they do. I feel like a new man up there. The Deadpan Mask helps me to control my drives, my putts and my temper. The fact that it doesn't reduce my score is unimportant. I'm still the best player in this asylum. Even Napoleon can't beat me!"*

Deadpan Mask of Bobby Jones, Sam Snead or Walter
  Hagen $7.77

Special models for women: Babe Didrickson, Patty
  Berg or Louella Parsons $9.99

For politicians: Deadpan Masks of Malenkov, Chiang-
  Kai-shek, Eisenhower or Churchill............................ $11.11

5: DANDY UTILITY GOLF BAG

Specially designed for forgetful folk, show-offs and maladjusted types, this latest wrinkle in bagdom is guaranteed to satisfy even the fussiest lunatic. Your friends will marvel, gasp and run for cover when you march up to the first tee with this juggernaut of golf bags!

Notice its outstanding features:

(A) *500 More Pockets!* The Dandy Utility Golf Bag is rigged to carry *everything!* Equipped with pockets of all sizes, this amazing bag can hold such items as: tees, keys, sweater, letters, socks, locks, powder, chowder, old scores, plus fours, keepsakes, Corn flakes, ladies' mules, folding stools, hot toddies and dead bodies.

(B) *Special percolator attachment for inveterate coffee drinkers.* This interesting gadget comes equipped with its own heating unit, plus a generous pocket for storing cups, saucers, old coffee grounds and antacid remedies.

(C) *Extra Special — Outboard Motor,* designed for pushing the bag over all kinds of terrain, while supplying heat for the Percolator. Guaranteed to ease the strain of walking, this wonderful machine uses practically no gasoline — since it runs on diesel oil only.

3: THE LITTLE GEM DIVING SUIT

Here's a dandy outfit for golfers who always slice into that pesky water hole. Too many sportsmen simply throw up their hands, throw down their clubs and throw in the sponge whenever they drive into deep water. Now you can salvage every ball you hit into the drink. Simply strap on the Little Gem Diving Suit, turn on the oxygen tank and then walk, do not run, into the water.

The model pictured above is designed for lakes, brooks, ponds, lagoons, coral reefs and shallow wells. For deeper areas such as oceans, seas, bays, inlets and canals, write for our Special Deep Water Kit, which comes equipped with more oxygen, heavier helmet, and a special waterproofed prayer book.

Knockdown price $245.89

GETTING A GOOD GRIP ON YOURSELF

As a grip is, a grip is, a grip is a valise.
My Hand Has Six Fingers.
                                        Gertrude Stein

Babe Didrickson, in her book *Championship Golf*, passes on this sage morsel of advice to all beginners:

"Your grip on the club is the only contact with the club."

This rule does not apply, however, to all golfers who prefer to grab the club with their toes, or hit the ball by clenching the club handle between their molars. Such players are considered show-offs and will not be discussed here. Anybody who chooses not to use his fingers for the game had better stick to soccer, potsy, or other sports involving the pedal extremities.

It's amazing how many golfing enthusiasts get all mixed up when grabbing a club. Impetuous beginners usually approach the stick in the manner of a homicidal maniac about to strangle his first customer. They commence to wrap their digits around the club with force and fervor, cracking their knuckles in desperation as though hell bent for squeezing sap out of a dry twig. Such gymnastics, of course, can only result in muscular tension, abrasions, blisters and scabs. The wiser, more experienced player will practice only the "Interlocking," or the "Overlapping" grips, long considered the best. The result of such effort cannot fail to produce lower scores, scabs, blisters, abrasions and muscular tensions.

A survey of the three most popular types of grip should prove helpful to everybody. Including myself.

Strange predicament of golfer who tried to change from the Interlocking Grip to the Overlapping Grip . . .

THE OVERLAPPING GRIP

This grip, originated by Cyrus K. Overlapping, affords most players the utmost in ease and comfort. The golfer should bear in mind that it took Overlapping many years to perfect his system of grabbing the club. The fruit of his labors involves the simple device of overlapping the little finger of the right hand on the index finger of the left. Left-handed players must reverse this routine and allow the little finger of the left hand to overlap the index finger of the right. Ambidextrous golfers often get confused and overlap thumbs with wrists. This state of affairs often leads to madness.

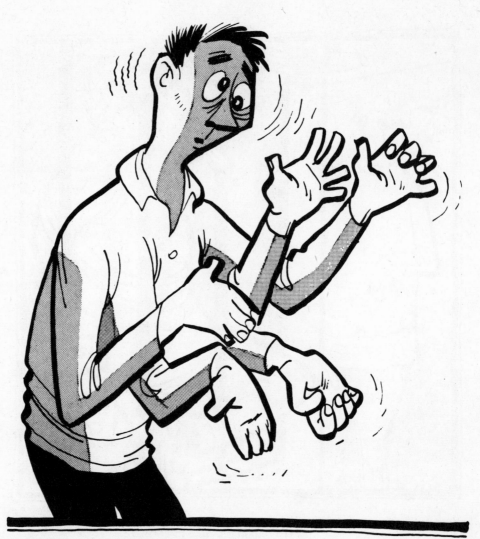

Peculiar mental state of beginning golfer after sampling various methods of gripping the club. . . . .

THE INTERLOCKING GRIP

Originally devised for players with small hands, this grip is popular with midgets, gnomes, dwarfs and elves. Since the latest census shows only .0045 per cent of these creatures in our population, we can skip this grip completely. Any midgets, gnomes, dwarfs and elves who want special instruction can buy my latest book, *Better Golf for Midgets, Gnomes, Dwarfs and Elves,* published in pocket size by The Leprechaun Press.

THE BASEBALL OR NATURAL GRIP

This is an unconventional grip, used by players with weak hands. Just seize the club as you would a ball bat. Now swing at the ball avidly, making sure that you aim directly over second base. This will avoid a slice, but may not net you a base hit. Always remember to slide for home.

THE LARIAR GRIP

After many years of intense study and diligent practice, I've devised a method for taking hold of a golf club that cannot fail to help all persistent bunglers at the game. When all other grips have failed, try mine:

(1) Put left hand on top of shaft.
(2) Put right hand alongside left hand.
(3) Squeeze the club.
(4) Swing.
(5) You missed? Swing again.
(6) Closer? Try it once more.
(7) Missed again?
(8) Reverse hands and grip club.
(9) Bring club down smartly against knee.
(10) Throw both pieces of club away.
(11) Throw the rest of clubs away.
(12) Go home.

"From now on, the course gets a bit tough . . ."

EXCLUSIVE! INSIDE STORY OF GOLF CLUBS EXPOSED!

WASHINGTON, D. C., Dec. 9, 1953. *Sensational investigation of golfing establishments yields bitter fruit! Red flags found flying on most greens! National pastime exposed as Kremlin plot by Cyrus O. Sludge!*

The nation's capitol erupted into small boils today when a new national menace was brought out into the open by Special Investigator Sludge, of the famous MacCartwheel Committee. Sludge is well known for his past performances in the field of research, having headed up such famous groups as:

(a) The Sludge Committee to Investigate Cotton Wadding in Aspirin Bottles.

(b) The Sludge Committee to Explore Drawstrings on Women's Girdles.

(c) The Sludge Committee on Small Wonders, Blunders and Thunders.

Now, after more than five years in limbo, Cyrus Sludge has returned to Washington to lay his bare facts on the table. As key witness on the MacCartwheel Committee to Investigate Golfing Clubs, Sludge faced the television cameras with great aplomb. His testimony, hot off the official records, is as follows:

QUESTION: State your name, and be brief.

ANSWER: My name is Cyrus O. Brief.

QUESTION: I thought your name was Sludge.

ANSWER: You asked me to be Brief, didn't you?

QUESTION: Stick to the facts, please. Is it true that you were hired as an undercover man to investigate golf clubs?

ANSWER: You hit that one right down the fairway, Senator.

QUESTION: What were you trying to prove?

ANSWER: Just this — that many American golf clubs are operating in an un-American fashion.

QUESTION: Ah? You mean — ?

ANSWER: Definitely! Surveys show that nine out of ten clubs feature red flags on every green.

Close-up study of $10.00 per year club member passing the time of day with $5,000 per year club member.

QUESTION: Marxian markers, eh? How about the pro's?

ANSWER: Most pro's are in the pink.

QUESTION: The club management knows this?

ANSWER: The club heads are positively stupid about what the score is, Senator. That's why almost all of them are in the red after every fiscal period.

QUESTION: How can you be so sure?

ANSWER: I got the inside stuff, right from the locker rooms.

QUESTION: How many of these subversive organizations did you join?

ANSWER: Only a few. My expense account wouldn't allow me to spread myself thin. Initiation fees are quite high these days.

QUESTION: Initiation fees? What are they for?

ANSWER: Nobody seems to know. My research shows that the exclusive clubs charge high fees to keep the middle class out.

QUESTION: And how about the middle class clubs?

ANSWER: Middle class clubs charge less, but just enough to keep the poor out.

QUESTION: And the poor clubs?

ANSWER: The poor clubs charge still less — but just enough to keep the paupers out.

QUESTION: What happens to the paupers?

Picture of patrons of public golf course, as it exists in mind of average private course member.

Graph showing relative size of average golf club member compared with the amount of beer he consumes each year.

ANSWER: Haven't you played a public course lately?

QUESTION: I'll ask the questions, Sludge! Now, what occurs after a member pays his initiation fee?

ANSWER: A strange phenomenon happens, Senator. Payment of the initiation fee permits the member to become eligible to pay other fees.

QUESTION: Such as?

ANSWER: Upon acceptance into any club, the member is expected to pay his yearly dues at once.

QUESTION: How much are these dues?

ANSWER: They range from $100 to $10,000, depending upon the wealth of the member and his ability to absorb shock.

QUESTION: The member pays without question?

ANSWER: Seasoned golf club members seem to enjoy the steady drain on their bankrolls. Since every other member is subjected to the same torture, the pain is somehow alleviated. The member's prestige in the club rises in direct contrast to the diminishing of his funds. Freud explains this as a type of masochism, or self-flagellation. But Freud is only theorizing. After all, he never played golf. His sex theories, however —

QUESTION: Watch your language, Sludge! Remember, we're on television. Now, after the club member pays his yearly dues, are there any expenses?

ANSWER: The member's financial worries only begin when he joins the club. After that, he is subjected to another tariff which drains his bank account at least once a week during the golfing season. This institution is known as The Saturday Night Dance.

QUESTION: Certainly a dance can't cost much, can it?

ANSWER: Are you kidding, Senator? Saturday Night Dances are festive affairs. Each member usually brings with him a "party" of friends.

QUESTION: Why is it called a "party"?

ANSWER: Because the member is giving it. No guest in the "party" ever reaches for the tab when the evening is over. At that time, the components of the "party" can be found in any of the following places:

(1) Taking a siesta in the Gentlemen's Lounge.
(2) Taking a siesta under a potted palm on the terrace.
(3) Studying astronomy with others of the "party"—beyond sight of the table, the host, or the bill.

QUESTION: And the member continues to take guests to each dance?

ANSWER: How can he stop? By this time he has gained a reputation as a *bon vivant*. To stop at this point would cause his wife and his children a great social shame.

QUESTION: How would that come about?

ANSWER: The member, once having ceased his Saturday Night Spending, falls at once into disrepute. He may be considered a failure in business, a bankrupt, a total loss, or a cheapskate. For this reason, he borrows heavily, puts on a brave front and continues to pour his money down the drain every Saturday night.

QUESTION: How long does this go on?

ANSWER: Nobody knows, since members of this type are usually the last to complain of scanty funds. They remain as "regulars" at "the old club" anywhere from five to fifty years.

Flash-bulb picture of club member in final few moments before the end of a Saturday Night Dance.

QUESTION: What happens after that?

ANSWER: The departing member usually moves to another part of the country to cover his confusion. There he will join another golf club, pay another initiation fee and start down another road to bankruptcy.

QUESTION: Hmmmmm — now, about these Saturday Night Dances. I've heard they're pretty — ah — wild affairs. Is this true?

ANSWER: Well, Senator, ummm — I — that is —

QUESTION: Stop hedging, Sludge! You attended many of these dances?

ANSWER: I did, sir. All in the line of duty, of course.

QUESTION: What time do they begin?

ANSWER: The usual Saturday Night Dance involves dinner first. This means that everybody warms up with a couple of cocktails. The atmosphere is rather gay and abandoned, the girls beautiful and spirited.

QUESTION: Keep talking. What about the ladies?

ANSWER: Charming, sir. Delightful —

QUESTION: You met many of them?

ANSWER: A reasonable number.

QUESTION: Pretty ones?

ANSWER: Quite.

QUESTION: Well built?

ANSWER: Quite.

QUESTION: Inebriated?
ANSWER: Quite.
QUESTION: Affectionate?
ANSWER: Quite.
QUESTION: Willing?
ANSWER: I refuse to answer, sir —
QUESTION: You must! Remember, Sludge, you're under oath! Let's have the details! I want names, addresses and telephone numbers —
ANSWER: I stand on my constitutional rights, Senator. I refuse to answer on the usual grounds — that I might incriminate myself!

... CURTAIN ...

IMPROVING A LIE IN THE ROUGH: Making good use of the car cushions.

HINTS AND TIPS YOU CAN LIVE WITHOUT

Ever since Gutenberg invented the art of fine print, kind-hearted golfing professionals have been treating the public to a steady outpouring of sympathetic prose, calculated to help the blundering duffer over the "hurdles" and "pitfalls" of learning, while gaining the expert author substantial bundles of "money" with which he can buy his "bread and butter" and sometimes "caviar."

This practice of counselling beginners has resulted in a new school of literature, called: *"The How-To-Do-It"* branch, a strange and inspiring type of prose halfway between fact and fiction. As the years wear on and the helpful hints become old and worn, the authors of this sort of wordage must turn to science-fiction for their inspiration, inventing weird problems that do not exist to satisfy the public craving for instruction.

Out of the welter of fancy facts in past golf books emerge strange gems of advice. A trip through a few recent Tables of Contents reveals such typical Chapter Headings as the following:

HOW TO FALL IN LOVE WITH YOUR FIVE IRON, or *Hints and Tips on the Right Way to Handle Your Clubs in Any Emergency, Including Insurrection, Riots and Migraine Headaches.*

HOW TO TWO-PUTT GREENS YOU FOUR-PUTTED YESTERDAY AND HOPE TO ONE-PUTT TOMORROW, or *Hints and Tips on the Stance and Grips for Standing and Gripping without Griping and Slipping.*

HOW TO DRIVE A SPOON, A WOOD, A CONVERTIBLE OR A JAGUAR, *with a Few Helpful Hints Concerning Hangnails, Toenails and Tight Shoes.*

HOW TO ANALYSE YOUR OPPONENT'S PLAYING STYLE, *with Special Commentary by Sigmund Freud, Krafft-Ebbing and Other Leading Psychiatrists.*

Any fool can see that this sort of pedantic pap is bound to wear down even the most avid neophyte. If such an abundant crop of stale thinking is allowed to persist, our golf courses will soon be crowded with a new breed of sportsmen, weird, crawling chaps who munch random wild berries, worms and passing beetles. It's about time somebody brought some common sense advice to the game. It's about time somebody faced up to the *real* problems, such simple things as breathing, looking, and walking. For the benefit of all newcomers within sound of my typewriter — here are the most basic helpful hints imaginable:

1: HOW TO GET INTO A GOLF COURSE

Most beginners imagine that they must go through a special ritual to get to the first tee and drive off. This just isn't so. To enter a golf course, simply walk to the front gate and look for signs. Most golf clubs have signs like this:

CRUMMY ELBOW HILLS

Members Only

GOLF AND BE DAMNED

This type of sign indicates a course limited to special club members who pay dues, spend money on liquor, and dance every Saturday night. To gain admittance to such an organization, you must either, (A) Try to join, (B) Get somebody to take you in, or (C) Pretend you're delivering groceries.

The easiest course to enter usually displays this type of sign:

BALDERDASH PUBLIC LINKS

Open To The Public

Admission: $1.98   Sundays and Holidays: $3.75

No Dogs Allowed

Children on Leashes Permitted

*Not Responsible For Any Cuts, Bruises or Lacerations
Obtained While on These Links!*

PLEASE REPLACE DIVOTS

Ladies in Bathing Suits Not Permitted on Greens!

WATCH YOUR GOLF BAG AT ALL TIMES

←Ladies' Room to Left   Men's Room to Right→

*Clubhouse Open for Luncheon, Dinner and Stag Parties —
Inquire at Desk for Special Rates*

NO PARKING!

Obviously, such a course is wide open to the public and will accept anybody equipped with the greens fee. Simply walk up to the desk, slap down your money and meander to the first tee, making sure to bring along sandwiches and hot broth for the five hour wait before you can tee off.

CLUB HEADS (Wooden): Chairmen of the Greens Committee.

Reaction of an average golfer after playing 36 holes of golf.

The same golfer's reaction to a request by his wife to walk to the corner grocery.

2: HOW TO WALK

The simplest way to develop good walking habits is by way of steady concentration and will power. Many beginners have a tendency to jump and sprint after the ball immediately following the shot. This is bad practice, poor strategy, and can result in a general weakening of all limbs before the 18th hole is reached.

To walk correctly, follow these simple rules:

(A) Lift right leg into air.
(B) Put right foot down on ground.
(C) Lift left leg into air.
(D) Drop it.
(E) Repeat with right leg, as in (A).
(F) Repeat with left leg, as in (C).
(G) Continue slowly.

3: HOW TO RUN

In case of emergencies, such as sudden hurricanes, squalls, hailstorms or blizzards, it may be necessary to run for cover. To do this simply repeat the process as outlined above, substituting the word *"quickly"* in (G).

121

4: HOW TO PLAY WITH STRANGE PARTNER (MAN)

Circumstances may sometimes arrange odd companions for the lone golfer who wanders the links. It is wise, when adjusting yourself for strange companionship, to memorize certain rules and regulations for putting the new partner at ease. The following scientific table should equip you for any type of personality:

IF HE SAYS . . .	YOU SAY . . .
"Want to play a round with me?"	"I'd be delighted."
"You go first — I'm a real duffer."	"Flattery will get you nowhere."
"That was a fine drive you just hit."	"Tsssk! Tsssk!"
"There I go — topping the ball again! I wonder why?"	"Your backswing seems loose."
"You've beaten me three straight holes. Wish you'd show me how to hold my hands."	"Try the interlocking grip."
"I feel fine with the new grip. Care to play for a buck a hole?"	"What have I got to lose?"
"Wow! Right on the green in two. Well, accidents can happen."	"Hmmmmmmm . . ."
"I'm getting better and better. I've been playing way over my head the last ten holes. Beginner's luck, I guess."	"Oh, sure."
"Looks like you owe me seventeen bucks, pal."	'Got change of a twenty?"
"Care to play again tomorrow?"	"Drop dead!"

5: HOW TO PLAY WITH STRANGE PARTNER (WOMAN)

IF SHE SAYS...   **YOU SAY...**

"Want to play a round with me?"   "Right here — in public?"

OVERLAPPING GRIP: A popular type of holding action.

GOLFING DICTIONARY

AMATEUR: Any golfer in a slow foursome just ahead.

ANGLE SHOT: A stroke shot from an unusual angle such as: (a) from behind a tree, (b) inside a culvert, or (c) a few yards in back of Marilyn Monroe.

APPROACH SHOT: The last shot to the green. You hope.

BALL: Small round object usually found in the deep woods.

BACKSWING: The process of carrying the club head up, out and behind the golfer in preparation for swinging out, down and behind the golf ball.

BAG: A large, ungainly item of luggage carried by caddies and cheapskates.

BIRDIE: A very small bird that sings whenever a golfer breaks par by one stroke.

BLAST: The sound a player makes when he shoots for the above-mentioned birdie—and misses.

CLUB: A device used by golfing enthusiasts for striking out at a golf ball. Clubs come in a variety of sizes, weights and lengths, depending upon the size of the player, the length of his arms and the weight of his bankroll.

CADDY: A small cad, usually left holding the bag.

DUB: This is simply the word "Bud" spelled backwards.

DUFFER: This is "Reffud" spelled similarly, but it means the same, no matter how you spell it.

DRIVE: The first stroke off the tee. (For variations, see: SLICE and HOOK.)
(For other variations, see: TOPPING and HEELING.)
(For still other variations, see: YOUR CLUB PRO, you fool, you!)

DORMIE: An old Scotch word meaning: Dead.

FAIRWAY: A long, narrow stretch of cut grass and lumpy earth, surrounded on all sides by deep woods, quicksand, boulders and lost golf balls.

FOURSOME: The quartette of snails, usually found immediately ahead of you on most golf courses.

FORE! A method of yelling at the above snails.

FOLLOW-THROUGH: A gesture involving club and arms at the end of a golf stroke that goes well.

GRIP: (See: INTERLOCKING GRIP or OVERLAPPING GRIP.) For other grips, visit your luggage store.

GREEN: A tiny patch of smooth lawn, usually overshot with your seven iron.

GROUND RULES: The small type on the back of your score card.

HOOK: A sharp left turn, usually made while driving.

HOLE-IN-ONE: A master stroke, normally followed by complete collapse, coma and delusions of grandeur.

HAZARD: A scientifically planned series of provoking encumbrances into which a golfer retreats to practice obscenity.

HANDICAP: A variation of the "Numbers Game."

LIE: The final resting place of every shot, called either "a bad lie" or a "good lie," depending upon the natural optimism of the player.

LINKS: A series of small greens joined together by connecting fairways, all of which lead inevitably back to the clubhouse and a further series of stories, joined together by connecting falsehoods.

MASHIE: A powerful iron generally used to mash the ball into the earth.

LOCKER ROOM: A large, enclosed room in which a series of lockers are used to contain a player's liquor supply.

NIBLICK: Another iron, employed for "nibbling" sections of turf from the fairway.

OUT-OF-BOUNDS: An expression created to indicate the legal area of the golf course, beyond which the player must either forfeit a stroke or create a suitable prevarication to cover his crookedness.

OVERLAPPING GRIP: A position of the hands used in holding a golf club generally taught by all professional instructors at the rate of $10.00 per finger.

PAR: A perfect score for each hole, devised by the architects who designed the course, none of whom ever played the game, damn them!

PIVOT: A method for adjusting the hips to accommodate the stroke, in the way that a rhumba swivel matches the rhythm of the music. This does not mean that a rhumba addict can hit the ball more than twenty yards, any more than a golf addict can rhumba twenty minutes.

PRO: Term of familiarity used to describe the best businessman in the club. He's clever enough to collect a fat fee for watching a fat millionaire flail his fat arms at nothing at all for an hour at a time.

PUTT: A short, tickling, tentative, teasing stroke intended to carry the ball into the cup.

The expression: "three-putt the green" means the golfer took three strokes to achieve his ends.

The term: "two-putt the green" means the player took two strokes for the same purpose.

The expression:

"YEEEEOOOWEEE!"

means that the contestant sank the putt in one fell swoop.

ROUGH: The section of weeds, furze, rocks, boulders, vines, veldt, jungle, swamp or tundra located on either side of the fairway as a lure for naturalist golfers who may wish to spend their time observing the local flora and fauna while searching for their golf balls.

SCORE CARD: A small slice of paper cleverly arranged to record golfing errors.

SLICE: A large hunk of air, usually cut by a golf ball at the end of its flight into unplayable acreage.

SPADE: A club used exclusively for ferretting in the earth.

STANCE: A scientific method by which the legs, feet, hips, arms, shoulders and toes are arranged in such a fashion as to make the golfer feel foolish at the tee.

STROKE: In medicine: a spasmodic twitching of the muscles, usually accompanied by excessive sweating, loss of breath, and palpitations of the heart.

In golf: ditto.

STYMIE: An ancient Scottish word meaning: *"You bastard, you!"*

TOURNAMENT: A golfing fiesta, in preparation for which club members spend thousands of dollars for lessons and new equipment, in order to attempt winning a small cup worth about ten bucks.

TRAP: A shallow hole, usually filled with sand and angry golfers.

WAGGLE: A movement of hips and buttocks, followed by the stroke.

WIGGLE: A feminine movement of the same sections of the anatomy usually followed by the men in the foursome behind.